JOBS IN OUR COMMUNITY

POLICE OFFICERS

on the Job

By Kate Rogers

KidHaven PUBLISHING

Published in 2017 by
KidHaven Publishing, an Imprint of Greenhaven Publishing, LLC
353 3rd Avenue
Suite 255
New York, NY 10010

Designer: Deanna Paternostro
Editor: Katie Kawa

Photo credits: Cover Blend Images - Hill Street Studios/Getty Images; pp. 5, 15, John Roman Images/Shutterstock.com; p. 7 Maciej Bledowski/Shutterstock.com; p. 9 Christian Mueller/Shutterstock.com; p. 11 robert cicchetti/Shutterstock.com; p. 13 Darrin Klimek/Getty Images; p. 17 Adwo/Shuttetstock.com; p. 19 Jupiterimages, Creatas Images/Thinkstock; p. 21 KellyNelson/Shutterstock.com; p. 23 Eric Broder Van Dyke/Shutterstock.com.

Cataloging-in-Publication Data

Names: Rogers, Kate.
Title: Police officers on the job / Kate Rogers.
Description: New York : KidHaven Publishing, 2017. | Series: Jobs in our community| Includes index.
Identifiers: ISBN 9781534521537 (pbk.) | ISBN 9781534521551 (library bound) | ISBN 9781534521544 (6 pack) | ISBN 9781534521568 (ebook)
Subjects: LCSH: Police–Juvenile literature.
Classification: LCC HV7922.R64 2017 | DDC 363.2–dc23

Printed in the United States of America

CPSIA compliance information: Batch #CW17KL: For further information contact Greenhaven Publishing LLC, New York, New York at 1-844-317-7404.

Please visit our website, www.greenhavenpublishing.com. For a free color catalog of all our high-quality books, call toll free 1-844-317-7404 or fax 1-844-317-7405.

CONTENTS

Police officers keep their community safe. They work hard!

Police officers have special police cars. These cars can go very fast.

You can hear police cars as they drive by. They have a loud siren.

Some police officers ride on horses.
They are called **mounted police officers.**

Police officers wear special clothes. These clothes are their **uniform**.

13

A police officer has a **badge**. This lets people know they are a police officer.

15

Police officers make sure people follow laws. Laws are important rules.

17

Sometimes two police officers work together. They are partners.

19

Some police officers have a dog for a partner.

21

Police officers are helpful and brave!

23

WORDS TO KNOW

badge

mounted
police officers

uniform

INDEX